*for Madeline*
*x.*

CW00410921

# WHEN *feathers* APPEAR

Your Guide to Finding Inner Peace
Through Challenging Times

By Jane Dunning

Copyright 2019: Jane Dunning

All Rights Reserved. Apart from any fair dealing for the purposes of research or private study, or criticism or review, as permitted under the Copyright, Designs and Patents Act 1988, this publication may only be reproduced, stored or transmitted , in any form or by any means, with the prior permission in writing of the copyright owner, or in the case of the reprographic reproduction in accordance with the terms of licences issued by the Copyright Licensing Agency. Enquiries concerning reproduction outside those terms should be sent to the publisher.

ISBN: 9781706351030

*I dedicate my book to Patricia Batty. Thank you for always believing in me, for the unconditional love, and for your friendship. I will love you forever, until we meet again x*

# CONTENTS

# INTRODUCTION

**D**uring your darkest nights of the soul, how good would it feel to know that you're never truly alone? Through times of struggle, hardship and the stresses of daily living, what if you knew that you were supported in ways unseen by the naked eye?

I had a happy childhood; indeed, none of my struggles in later life can be attributed to my upbringing. Yet life threw many curveballs that left me feeling broken and - at times - wishing for anything but to be here. That's the beauty of life. No matter your intentions, no matter how much you try to do things 'right', the universe will have ways of seemingly throwing you off course, only for you to find yourself on the exact path that was meant for you. This is certainly true for me.

Every hurdle and obstacle that threatened my sense of self and safety awakened something innate within me and brought me closer to my true essence and the gifts that resided there. Every experience brought a

1

newfound strength and resilience that kept me going and moving forward, despite my desire to retreat and hide away. And through everything, I knew with 100% clarity and certainty that I was being guided, no matter how lonely I felt along the way.

*When Feathers Appear* was born from a realisation that a higher source - angels - were guiding me through my life and its challenges. At my lowest ebb, a small feather would randomly appear, or I would look at up at the sky and see angel wings for clouds, and with them came an unspoken message: you are supported. I knew that I wasn't alone. And I learned to trust each experience as it unfolded, moment to moment. I trusted that every challenge that was being presented to me, no matter how difficult, was for my highest good; our breakdowns often lead to our biggest breakthroughs and healing when we allow ourselves to see through the experience.

It is my intention with this book to give you hope and comfort in your darkest and loneliest times. I want you to start to notice and trust the signs, as well as the whispers of your soul and intuition, guiding you through your challenges. All the answers lie within you; sometimes, you need a little help to find them.

I'd also like angels to enter the mainstream and become a 'normal' part of modern life. Spirituality does not need to be considered 'woo-woo' or limited to the psychically gifted. We are all spiritual beings at our core, regardless of whether we have a spiritual practice or label ourselves as such, and the love and support from the angels is available to us all; they do not discriminate.

Use this book as a trusted companion. Read it from cover-to-cover, or dip in and out to receive the message that you need to hear at that moment. However you choose to use this book, let it be your guide towards inner peace.

Fourteen-year-old girl, sat on the edge of her bed
What was that noise, was it inside her head?
Muffled laughter from the corner of the room
She felt fear, a cold sense of doom

"Stop it," she cried, "just go away"
Give me some peace, just for a day
Then SNAP went the picture, it fell to the floor
That was it – she was out of the door

She walked in the lounge; her mum looked up
She was having a brew, from her favourite cup
"Mum, I am scared ... this picture, it fell off the wall"
"Darling it's nothing, just an old hook, that was all"

The girl not convinced, she sat on the chair
Why wouldn't mum listen? She needed to share
Time passed by and the house calmed down
No more spooks, there wasn't a sound

Until that dark night when the girl went to bed
What was that? Was it inside her head?
Crackle laughter, it came loud and clear
A shadow from the corner, started to appear

*Just go away* she cried to herself
Then crash went the ornament, it fell from the shelf
Turning away, trying to sleep that night

It's hard when your body, is racked in fright

Learning to live and squashing her fears
The spook still came for a couple more years
The older she got, the less she saw
The spook wanted energy; she gave it no more …

**– *It Went Bump in the Night***

# 1.
# IT WENT BUMP IN THE NIGHT

*"I want to sing like the birds sing, not worrying about who hears or what they think."* ~ Rumi

**W**e are born to live as the fullest expression of our whole selves - physically, spiritually and emotionally - yet through life events, trauma and conditioning, we typically disconnect from the essence of who we are. Much dis-ease can be attributed to abandoning and forgetting our true self as we seek external means to fill the void. However, who we are never leaves us but is lying dormant, waiting to be re-awakened. As the angels guide us, leaving signs and clues pointing us back into the direction of our soul, we can re-connect with those lost parts and unleash our unique gifts and soul essence into the world.

I had a blessed childhood and felt loved from the moment I was born. My parents had me young - Mum was 20 while Dad was 25 - and I wasn't planned. My mum didn't know she was pregnant. While lying on a beach in her bikini, she felt what she assumed to be my dad tickling her. "Stop tickling me," she said. It wasn't Dad. This was the first moment Mum felt me fluttering in her tummy.

The moment I was born, there was an instant recognition, a deeply spiritual connection that had traversed four generations. My mum and dad wanted more children but unfortunately this wasn't meant to be, so I was an only child and feel very lucky to have been born against the odds. I was adored and well cared for; I couldn't have wished for a better childhood and more loving parents and grandparents.

As a child, I had pretend friends and always saw things in the shadows. "Who is that man at the top of the stairs?" I once asked when I was little. Aged thirteen, my granddad died. This was my first experience of death. I didn't attend the funeral but stayed at home with my nanny Pat, waiting for people to arrive for the wake. I was distraught. I didn't want people around me grieving. As an only child, I was used to having a monopoly on attention and wasn't used to sharing people. I felt as though Grandad was *my* Grandad and only I was allowed to mourn and alone with my parents, no one else. Grief turned to anger, and I became a surly teenager – my "cow phase" began.

Soon, things would start to happen around the house. Things would fall off the kitchen worktops, and otherwise sturdy items would randomly fall. This never scared me. "It's only Grandad," I'd say. Sensing his presence felt so natural and normal to me. It felt comforting. It never occurred to me that this gift was quite unusual and that others couldn't see or feel the things that I did.

We moved houses when I was 15, and at this time I attracted a poltergeist which scared the living daylights out of me! Windows would close all by themselves and pictures would fall off the wall. The radio would turn itself on, and I would hear footsteps chasing me down the stairs. I wanted to get away; I was starting to get scared. I wanted whoever it was to go away and leave me alone; this didn't feel like such an appealing gift anymore. We lived in a four-bed house so had plenty of spare rooms for me to sleep in to get away, albeit the 'spook' followed me no matter which room I switched to. I kept telling myself, *I know it's only Grandad, he wouldn't hurt me.* Even though a part of me knew it wasn't him.

For my 16th birthday, I was gifted a beautiful Victorian bracelet from my parents with my name engraved on it. It was made from very heavy silver, and I wore it all the time, even in bed. One night while drifting off to sleep, a thought entered my mind. What if I lose my jewellery in the night? I quickly checked my wrist, and sure enough, the bracelet was still there, as were my necklace and earrings. Satisfied that my mind was at ease, I fell asleep. During the night, I awoke with a start. My heart was racing, and I felt panicked. I reached for my necklace and earrings – they were still there. But my bracelet was gone. It had completely vanished, never to be seen again. This was the moment that I shut down spiritually. I was petrified; this 'gift' was starting to feel more like an unwanted and unnecessary burden that terrified me.

When I was 18 we moved again, and everything calmed down. I got a job, enjoyed going out with friends, had a boyfriend and started to live - for want of a better word - a 'normal' life. My spiritual gift started to fade, locked away in the depths of my soul and stayed there, for many many years, until a series of events cracked it wide open, as you will discover later in this book.

\*\*\*

We are born into this world as open channels. Young children are naturally psychic and sensitive to the energies around them and can see entities that others cannot. Over time, these abilities become desensitised or shut down completely, primarily due to conditioning and trauma. The most sensitive of children often carry these gifts through childhood, adolescence and into adulthood - until something happens that causes them to shut down. Perhaps you recognise this in yourself. Maybe you saw spirit - perhaps deceased loved ones - or heard voices. Perhaps your intuition was incredibly strong, or you could read the energy of a room as soon as you walked in. You may have been able to feel the emotions of others without them uttering a word. Maybe you had an infinite capacity for unconditional love, yet something happened, and you closed off your heart.

As children, the ability to see, hear and feel the unseen is the most natural thing in the world – until a child is told that it's not. Intuition is something available to us all and can come in many forms, yet the mainstream still favours human logic and intelligence. History has shown us that many people have been institutionalised for seeing or speaking to 'ghosts' or hearing voices, and while there is more awareness now, spirituality is still feared, mocked or stigmatised, especially by the non-believers (or those who don't understand). As a child, if your abilities were frowned upon or you internalised a lot of shame because of them, then at some point you will likely have closed off that part of you. The voice of the adults around you became yours; you stopped trusting your intuition.

However, it's not too late to reconnect with your true essence and reawaken your innate gifts and spirituality. When life presents challenges, much of our suffering comes from disconnecting from our spiritual selves and the innate wisdom and resilience that can see us through tough times. When we disconnect from our heart and soul, we will inevitably feel pain. Of course, opening up this part of you doesn't mean that you're going to start seeing dead people or communicating with spirit - not everyone's spirituality and unique gifts manifest in this way. But it does mean reconnecting with the essence of you that was born into this world. The essence of who you were as a child (and still are beneath it all). It means tuning into and learning to trust your intuition and inner compass - relearning to trust yourself - and paying closer attention to the signs around you that are guiding you along the way.

We are all souls having a human experience which comes with many trials and tribulations as well as gifts. Whether you have a gift to heal through your hands or your words, for example, you are here to actualise that gift. We live in a world of polarity, and everyone has something to bring to the table.

However, when our gifts don't align to what is considered 'normal', or we have been conditioned to follow a more capitalist path because of modern society, we often abandon them and, in doing so, ourselves. When we abandon ourselves, life feels harder, heavier and more of a struggle. Stepping into your whole self, gifts and all, doesn't mean that life won't throw curveballs at you: it will. The nature of the human experience is such that we will experience pain; we cannot bypass it. But the more aligned we are to our true essence and who we came here to be, the greater our resilience through difficult times and the closer we get to finding inner peace.

Our gifts are evident when we are small children. It could be the role we consistently assumed during role-play, e.g. a teacher, or it could be hours singing and dancing around the house. Maybe you could paint and draw without judgement or attaching yourself to the outcome but did so purely to bring joy and colour to your life and the life of others. Perhaps you were a real chatterbox and a natural leader – until your chatty-ness and 'bossiness' became an inconvenience and shamed out of you. When we are young, we gravitate towards what is natural and innate. Joy is our sign-post. Our soul is alive, and we indulge its wants and needs. By the time we are seven, conditioning and disapproval from external sources take a firm grip, and we spend less time doing the very thing that brings us the most joy. Sometimes we experience trauma or deep shame and the thing that we loved to do no longer feels safe, so we abandon it and shy away from it completely. Yet throughout our lives, this thing will keep calling us, a deep yearning that resides from deep inside our heart, not our head. You may have abandoned it, but the call never abandons you.

That moment when you feel most at peace and 'at home' is your connection to your true nature. The things that you do when you lose all sense of time are those moments when your soul feels most aligned. We can all access our true nature, even when we're experiencing our darkest moments. Have you ever felt so lost, so alone and ready to escape yet the briefest glimmer of hope broke through? Perhaps you've been in a dark place yet had fleeting moments of inner peace and calm. Insight is always available to us; wisdom speaks and helps us see a new perspective. Angels are a way of wisdom speaking to you, calling your attention to the answers that are already inside you. Their presence, particularly in times of need, reminds you that you're safe, you belong, and you're not alone.

You are here to be who your soul desires. A soul denied its most authentic expression becomes lost and starved and will crave fulfilment. Quite often, we seek fulfilment externally, finding ways to feel safe and connected, even though the very ways we meet our needs are often those that further disconnect us from our soul. Addiction and depression are both symptoms of an unexpressed soul, as we fill the void through instant gratification and ways that give us a high, no matter how brief. Alcoholism, shopping and sex are some of the ways that we meet our need for connection. After the high comes a low, as we spiral downwards, seeking that feeling which we call 'home', looking more and more outside of ourselves to find it. I spent many years feeding my soul with food, as you will discover in chapter 8, before realising that everything I sought was inside me all along. By turning inwards and listening to the whispers, while also paying attention to the clues and signs from the angels around us, the more connected we become to our true nature, the part of us that is everything we seek and can never be broken.

Take a moment to consider your gifts. What part of your childhood have you abandoned? Before you reached the age of seven, what brought you the most joy? What were your 'superpowers' that have long been dismissed or forgotten?

Consider all the qualities that feel natural and innate and require little effort, as well as bringing you joy and a feeling of being alive. We're programmed to believe that life and work should be hard, so anything that feels easeful and flows often feels self-indulgent and a luxury we don't deserve, so we stop valuing, prioritising or pursuing it.

Now consider your life and the gift of the human experience. While humans share many similarities, we are all unique. Only you can be the authentic expression of you. Only you are here to be you. External influences and your own thinking may distract and deter you from being who you came here to be, but your path is yours and yours alone. The journey can be bumpy and take many unexpected (and unwanted) twists and turns, yet the lessons you learn along the way are part of your human and soul evolution. Your angels are here to guide you towards your innate gifts and wisdom. No matter how long or arduous the journey, you are never alone.

## How to reconnect with your soul's essence

Your soul is the one thing that never lies to you and is always with you – your most faithful companion. Yet we spend so much time ignoring the whispers and nudges, instead allowing our head to dominate and using outside influences to guide us. Reconnecting with your soul is about reconnecting with your true inner being and, as a result, aligning with your purpose, passions and the part of you that makes you feel whole.

**Meditate.** Bring your awareness to your body and breath and find the space and stillness within. If you have a particularly busy mind, start by meditating for 5-minutes, taking each day at a time and gradually increasing your meditation time. Audio guided meditations can be helpful if you find it difficult to quieten your mind yourself. If meditation isn't for you, consider an activity that helps you to drop into a meditative state – something that connects you with that stillness within. For some people this can look like painting, carrying out a repetitive task, or even doing something as mundane as the ironing or washing up. During meditation observe your thoughts – without judgement – and listen to the voice of your higher self as it comes through.

**Be in nature.** Nature is an excellent way to quieten your mind, particularly at times of stress and anxiety. Being in nature promotes presence as we slow down, clear our mind and become more aware of the beauty of our surroundings. While in nature, be present to all of your senses – what do you see, hear, feel, taste and smell? What are the intuitive thoughts coming into your awareness? Many of us have disconnected from nature yet we are nature – we are created from the same source - which is why nature can be profoundly healing.

**Quieten your mind** for a few minutes, set a 5-minute timer, then write a list using free-flow writing of all the things that you love. The idea is not to over think or over analyse but merely let your pen and unconscious mind do the thinking for you. A good time to do this is upon waking when your brain is still in the alpha stage – the gateway to the subconscious mind. The things written on your list – especially those nearest the top – are those that feed your soul and leave you feeling aligned and alive.

## LET'S REFLECT:

- Only you are here to be you
- When you feel most at peace and at home, you are connected to your soul.
- Insight is always available to you even in the darkest of times.
- The more aligned you are to your true essence and who you came here to be, the greater your resilience through difficult times.

- Angels remind you that you're safe, you belong, and you're not alone.

He looked so sad as he spoke to his wife
Knowing he was about to destroy her life

The memories they made, the laughter and tears
The pain the joy the sacrifice for so many years

Their marriage should last a lifetime –
that was going to be the plan

But life turned around and said to him
you've done enough you've done everything you can

*– Marriage Ends*

## 2.

# WE GREW UP TOGETHER

*"That which does not kill us, makes us stronger."* ~
*Friedrich Nietzsche*

**W**e are all intuitive by nature, yet our ego will have us believe otherwise. Such is the dominant paradigm that favours the ego, we learn to stop trusting our intuition; however, it never truly evades us. Your intuition is always guiding you; you need to tune in and listen. Every experience we have in life is an opportunity to follow our head or our heart. Sometimes it's necessary to integrate both. However, our head typically dominates, and we make decisions from a place of fear and our human need for safety and certainty. Quite often, our need to feel safe leads to more pain.

Aged 22, I left home. My mum didn't want me to go, but I was determined; I needed my independence, and I was excited for this next chapter in my life. I found a room to rent in a shared house. It was only a box room but met my basic needs so, three weeks after viewing, on a cold, January night, I moved in. A day later, I heard the door open. A tall, dark and extremely handsome man walked in. "Oh, you must be the new lodger," he said. "You must be the other lodger," I replied. The attraction on my part was instant and – I hoped – mutual. We spent many nights sharing carpet picnics and listening to jazz music. Before long, our relationship flourished, and we moved into a small flat in South East London.

We renovated the flat, making it our own. It had a small balcony leading to a shared garden which was a game changer for me! I got my first cat, a big ginger tom called Arthur, and I really felt as though I was living my best life – even down to the avocado green corner bath! I was unbelievably happy. The years passed and in 1989 I married the man of my dreams.

The wedding was beautiful. It was the perfect fairytale wedding followed by a honeymoon in Skiathos. We were incredibly close, had a wonderful circle of friends and, on the whole, had a great life together. My husband was gregarious, flamboyant, friendly, and the perfect host at dinner parties. We ran a business together, would shop together, and basically did everything together. We were best friends who were growing up as well as growing together. It seemed the most natural step to bring two beautiful children into the world.

When Daisy and Edward were ten and seven, we made a decision to relocate to Yorkshire and start a property renovation and rental company together. We would be living close to my in-laws. By this point, my parents were retired and were used to being so close and spending so much time with us. I didn't have the heart to tell them our plans, so I organised everything without saying a word. In fact, I didn't tell anyone. I tied up loose ends to prepare for what was going to be a significant life change. I found a perfect school, a house, everything we needed to resettle into our new lives.

Then the day came to tell my parents. I was dreading this moment. I felt as though I was about to rip out their hearts. Currently, they were only 20-minutes down the road, but here I was, about to tell them that I was moving a 4-hour journey away. I shared the news. There was a moment of silence.

My dad spoke first. "If you're moving, we're coming with you!" This was music to my ears. It had never occurred to me that they might want to up sticks and join us. Everything was falling nicely into place!

In the winter of 2004, with two children, cats and a rabbit in tow, I moved to Yorkshire. My husband had unfinished business to attend to and I had to enrol the children into their school. We decided he would join us six months later. My parents were still in the process of selling their house, so I had to wait for them too. I felt incredibly lonely. This was a fresh new start with fresh new opportunities, but I hadn't prepared for the loneliness. My in-laws were close by but, having seen them only a handful of times a year, they didn't know the real soul-bearing me, only the snapshot of who I was on their brief visits. The children settled in at school, and I slowly got to know people. The loneliness began to subside, and I started putting the feelers out for a job. But I missed my husband and parents terribly.

In June, my husband was able to join us in Yorkshire. I was so excited to see him. I opened the door, full of love and gratitude for him being here but ... he was different. I barely recognised him. Something about his energy and appearance had changed entirely. He was stand-offish, never fully present and seemed distracted somehow. He wasn't the man I knew. Then the day came. The day that shook my world and flipped my whole life upside down. I remember the moment exactly.

It was an evening in July. My husband was sat in the kitchen, wearing a blue shirt, his head in his hands. He was struggling with something, a decision. His pain was palpable. What have I done wrong? I thought. He hadn't been the same since he'd come to

Yorkshire. He'd been distant, and I surmised that it must have been because of me. I sensed a difficult conversation coming on, so I asked my daughter to take her brother upstairs. Then I asked him directly what was wrong, why he'd been acting strange since he'd moved in.

"You don't know the half of it," he said, sounding like a man with the weight of the world on his shoulders.

"What half don't I know?" I asked. Had something bad happened? Was he having an affair? "You need to tell me - right now - because I'm blaming myself for your misery."

Then he crumbled. A broken man, the weight becoming too much to bear. He looked at me, like a lost little boy, with tears in his eyes.

"Jane, I'm gay."

Life stopped. Everything became a hazy blur as the world seemed to move in slow motion while the walls came crashing down. I felt unsteady on my feet.

"How long?" I asked.

"All my life," he said.

Slowly, piece by piece, things started to make sense.

The way he would go for a drive at all hours of the night. The way he disappeared for 7-hours in New York and couldn't account for his time. He was my best friend. How could I have not seen the signs? Had our whole relationship - our entire life - been a complete lie? I'd felt loved by him, I knew his love was genuine, and despite the pain and anguish which was to follow, I'm so grateful that he fathered my children – two strong individuals who have become the best of both of us. I can only imagine the battle that must have been going on inside his head for all those years.

We continued to share the same house, albeit in separate bedrooms. I needed time to understand what had become of my marriage. My parents and close friends had been told but to the outside world we were just another married couple who were going through a rough patch.

At times it was difficult, and we'd find ourselves at loggerheads, screaming and shouting at one another. We were both hurting in our own way and projecting our pain onto the other. It would be another year before we told our children that their father was a gay man, so we did our best to stay calm in their presence. We felt they were too young to understand and wanted to spare them from our pain as much as we could.

When the time did come to tell them, I had no idea what to do. I couldn't find the right time or the right words. I decided to write it down. I grabbed a pen and paper and started writing. The words flowed. It was as though someone else had taken control of the pen and the perfect message came out. The message flowed through me, not from me. I knew it wasn't me writing; the angels were supporting me. The following day I told them. My words were loving and supportive, the message clear. After, as I held my heard high looking far braver than I felt, he said, "Jane, you are stronger than me. I could never have done what you just did." My reply was simple: "Mother love took over." I had the opportunity to control the situation and salvage some of my own dignity. It had to be done on my terms, my way, and – looking back – with the help of the angels.

***

Coming to terms with a situation that has hurt you beyond all recognition of yourself is one of the most courageous things to do. It takes a strength so deep and powerful. As humans, when we are at rock bottom, we wonder if we will ever find a way out. The emotions are beyond our normal comprehension and we feel despair and depression.

The truth is, we all have an innate resilience that we can draw upon at any time, however, many of us try to avoid our pain and push it down, causing it to have power over us. What you resist persists, after all. Take a moment to think back to a difficult time in your life. How did you overcome it? The inner resilience that got you through that experience is still within you and can be pulled upon at any time.

## How to work through pain and suffering

**Acknowledge all of the emotions** as they arise. Feeling your feelings is not a weakness; it's a strength. The only way out is through and often the most uncomfortable. We have been blessed as humans to experience a whole spectrum of emotions and indeed we are meant to feel them all. Much of our suffering is as a consequence of not allowing ourselves to feel fully. A negative emotion will not attract more negativity into your life; it is merely a signpost of how you're feeling in this moment and must be honoured. Acknowledgment of these feelings is the first step towards becoming stronger. Ignoring them is a sure-fire way to remain stuck in your suffering.

**We all have an inner voice** that is often somewhat of a bully. Be aware of this voice sabotaging your progress as you claw your way out of the pit of despair; it will try to knock you back down. It takes a huge amount of strength to reprogram your inner voice and change the words that are speaking to you. Quite often, a negative relationship – whether with a parent, friend or partner – becomes our inner voice, the voice of the person who most criticised us or left us feeling unsafe. Be aware of who the voice really belongs to and if you know you're carrying someone else's emotional baggage, silently and energetically give it back.

Of course, we have another inner voice: our intuition. This is where it becomes really helpful to look around you for the signs and messages from the angels so that you can start to discern the difference between the two voices.

**There are many resources** and self-help books available to help us when we are at our lowest ebb as well as different healing modalities and therapies. Find what resonates and works for you, being mindful of old familiar patterns resurfacing as you go through the different stages of healing. What worked for me was journaling my highs and lows, often ranting in red pen, screaming and crying while I did it. Many years later when I rediscovered my journal,

I read it and then, knowing I had grown stronger from the experience, I destroyed it. It felt good! Even now when I find myself spiralling downwards, I take pen to paper and write down my thoughts, often in the form of automatic writing to tap into my subconscious and allow the angels' guidance to come through.

## LET'S REFLECT:

- Facing your pain is one of the bravest things to do.
- You are innately resilient, even if it doesn't feel like it at times.
- The inner resilience that got you through tough times is still within you.
- Discern between your two inner voices – your inner critic and your intuition. Trust the signs.

I was a Moth to the firelight it shone too bright to see
Blinded by its beauty I lost a bit of me.

I danced and sang my heart out
My shadow dancing there
Feeling young and beautiful
I embraced the fires flare

I knew it wouldn't hurt me –
This fire was my friend
How could something so beautiful
Be my spirits end

*– The Moth*

3.

# THE PROUD MAN

*"The wound is the place where the Light enters you."*
*~ Rumi*

As humans we have a need for connection and belonging. We gravitate towards other humans and sometimes feel an instant connection towards them, a feeling so strong we call it love. It feels like love: the endorphins are the same as love and our emotions and physical body allow us to believe it's love. However, when this relationship is challenged and the person you believed loved you changes, we realise it wasn't love but infatuation on your part, and a controlling, unhealthy, all-encompassing possession on theirs. You see a clink in their armour, and you try to escape. The monster appears, staring back at you with cold hatred in its eyes. Yet, you're compassionate and hopeful heart stays, a pattern that is repeated in many different relationships.

A couple of years later I met another man. a big, burly builder from Leeds. He was the complete polar opposite to my first husband. Perhaps on some psychological level, I thought someone completely different would reduce the risk of being hurt again. We soon became a couple, and I poured every ounce of love into my new relationship. All the love I still had inside me I redirected into this new man; I gave myself to him completely.

As part of my divorce settlement, I received half of the value of the properties plus cash. I rented out properties and my new partner managed them. It seemed the perfect arrangement, what with him being a builder. Life started to feel good again. In the pit of my stomach, I knew something wasn't entirely right, but I chose to ignore those early alarm bells – a trade-off for the happy and comfortable life that I was creating.

In 2007, I made the worst mistake of my life: I married this man on the rebound. Now, of course, hindsight is a wonderful thing, and because things happened since that day, it's easy for me now to declare it as being the worse mistake. But intuition had been speaking to me the whole time. Angels had been giving me signs and clues, but I'd ignored them. So, against my better judgement, marrying him still made the most sense at the time.

The wedding reception went relatively well. Everyone was in good spirits. Then, when it was time for the speeches, the best man stood up. In front of my family and children, he started making cruel, disrespectful and inappropriate jokes about my ex-husband and the fact that he was gay while my new husband wasn't. I was mortified and shocked that my husband was happily laughing along, while my children were sat there, looking confused and embarrassed. They didn't deserve their father's life to be a source of ridicule; neither did I. It was my previous life, and one I was still hurting from.

The marriage was consummated in the morning, but I was still shocked and angry. "How could you have let him say those things?" I cried. My new husband shrugged, nonchalantly. "He was drunk! We do silly things when we're drunk," he said in his friend's defence. I still wasn't convinced of my new husband. A dark, sinister hole was forming in my mind and I could feel myself falling into it.

We went on a trip to Holy Island for our honeymoon. Up until then, our sex-life had been great! Then it all changed, and all those little hints and nudges that something was off came to fruition. I made a sexual advance, as you do in a loving relationship. He looked at me. Something shifted in his eyes, like a cloud of darkness had swept in. They looked empty and cold, cruel even.

"I don't do fat birds!" he grimaced. "You're mine now; I own you!"

I felt so rejected as a woman, still coming to terms with the rejection from my previous husband which was no fault of my own. This man knew exactly how to hurt me. I had been recovering from a period of anorexia and had struggled with my weight most of my adult life. And now, here I was, with a man I didn't know at all and who admitted he would rather masturbate to girl-on-girl porn than have sex with me!

The more controlling he was, the more trapped I became. Now, people often wonder why women don't leave abusive partners. I can tell you this: when coercive control - as was my experience - takes hold, it permeates to the core of your very being and leaves scars that run deep. You start to lose all sense of self, stop trusting yourself, and your self-esteem chips away more and more. You build dependency on that person, becoming entangled in a need to feel loved and oscillating between the abuse and those good, happier times, the good always outweighing the bad. The abuse becomes familiar and often feels safer than being alone. And when money is involved, or lack thereof on my part, it can be tough to leave.

Meanwhile, the abuser presents a very different - and credible - picture to the world.

We went on a family holiday with the children. He was a heavy drinker - verging on alcoholism - so spent most of it drunk. The drunker he became, the more emotionally abusive he would be. I would get drunk with him; it was the only way I could cope. Before long, he began to mistreat my children, trying to control them and their behaviour, having very high and unrealistic expectations about who they should be and how they should present themselves to the world.

When my son was 9, we had a dinner party. My son came downstairs wrapped in a towel, having just got out of the shower. My husband started shouting at him to admit he'd done something wrong (when he hadn't), trying to humiliate him and make him look feeble in front of our guests. The abuse was never physical, but it was emotional, the kind of traumatic experience that children take into their adult lives. They even called him Dad. He was, after all, the only consistent male presence in their lives at the time. Their father had gone to Brazil, which had deeply hurt them, and my husband used it to drive a rift between them and their dad. Regretfully, I did too.

I felt so trapped. I wanted to leave. I needed to protect

my children. But I couldn't go anywhere. The mortgage wasn't in my name – he had control of all of the rental properties and finances. I was penniless. In 2009, I was declared bankrupt and lost everything. The mortgage couldn't be paid because he had mismanaged the rental properties and splurged all the cash, so no rent was coming in. I was stuck in a bind. Not only was I being emotionally abused but financially abused too yet needed to keep a roof over our heads. My children needed some level of security. The environment wasn't safe, but neither would homelessness be.

The catalyst finally came in the shape of my daughter. When she was born, we didn't have an amazing connection. The bond wasn't natural or instant, as the romantic notion of parenting and childbirth would have us believe. My mum was worried. Being an only child, I'd never experienced sibling rivalry or having to share love and affection. This gave me a sense of entitlement and superiority; all the attention was mine, always. I didn't know what to do with my daughter or how to feel about her. She was someone who my parents would share their love with and, on some level, take the attention away from me.

One day, my three-week-old daughter was in her travel seat. My dad walked in. "Hello twinkle," he said. I pounced on him, indignant as I said, "She's not your twinkle, I am!" From that moment upon hearing myself, my motherly love came flooding in. I was overwhelmed by the purest of love, so powerful and protective. My whole perception of motherhood change in an instant. I finally understood the hype. I would gladly lay down my life for this little human. My baby. My daughter. This little innocent baby was not a threat to my own security or safety. She was to be protected, loved and cherished. Bringing the truth of my fear of rejection out of the shadow and into the light had allowed it to lose some of its control. I began to understand unconditional love and how love grows, not divides.

My new husband didn't understand unconditional love, but I'd been so open and infatuated with him that he knew everything about me, even my daughter's birth story. When Daisy was 16, he and I were arguing. In a spit of rage, he turned to her and said, "Your mother didn't love you when you were born." Her face crumpled. She looked anguished; I don't think I've ever seen a child look so troubled. She ran into her bedroom, sobbing.

That was it. That was the moment. "Fuck you; you have no idea what you've done!" I said. No more. It's one thing hurting me, quite another hurting my child. My child, not his! He had no right to treat her like that.

That would be the last time he would ever get to abuse my kids and me.

I went into my daughter's room and laid next to her, consoling her. I explained Post-Natal Depression and how I did love her - really love her - but at the time, I didn't know how. Thank goodness there's more awareness of PND these days! Watching her looking so upset and rejected brought back all of those old familiar feelings of rejection. It's like the fog cleared and I suddenly saw everything with crystal clear clarity. "I'm going to fix this," I said. And this time I meant it.

At 6 am one morning, while my husband was still asleep, I drove to my parents' house. I couldn't live like this anymore. We were all treading on eggshells, all afraid and becoming shadows of our former selves, our lights dimming. I had to leave. But I needed help. Were the angels nudging me to get up and go that morning? Possibly. Something forced me to wake up! And now, finally, I was listening.

I arrived at my parents' house. "Dad," I said, "I have to leave him. What's stopping me is money." My parents knew things had been difficult, but they didn't understand the extent. Abusers are master manipulators, after all. But they'd seen me fade over time. They'd seen their grandchildren's spirit slowly diminishing. They knew something was wrong.

"Don't worry about the money," Dad said later than same day. I plucked up as much courage as I could muster, we left. I took my children back to my parents' house with nothing but one suitcase and a few of the kids' belongings to show for our lives.

***

Sometimes in our lives, things happen that force us to question the validity of our intuition. Yet, our intuition never lies. Many times I've been shown a different path, a different insight, yet I've ignored the guidance presented to me. Sometimes it's safer to bide your time until the moment is right, particularly if you are in any kind of abusive relationship like I've experienced. Sometimes you're not ready to see the truth of a situation even though when looking back, it's clear as day to see. And sometimes it's about bringing greater focus onto your awareness and paying closer attention to the signs that are presented to you.

I do not doubt that through everything, the angels were there, either leaving signs and clues or simply holding and supporting me through my darkest days. I honestly don't know how my experiences didn't completely break me. Something was guiding me through, towards my inner resilience and strength so that I could come out stronger, clearer and ready to take action.

We can be so entangled in our circumstances that walking away or taking immediate action isn't always the safest, easiest or logical thing to do at the time – there are always going to be external factors and barriers that are outside of your control. But rest assured, the angels are there with you, helping to guide you towards a solution and to support you when you're ready to take that next step.

At times you may sense a presence, and it feels calming and comfortable. Perhaps you may see something at the corner of your eye, yet nothing is visibly there. You may get a deep sense of inner peace, in spite of your pain. And maybe a small white feather appears by your feet while you're sat drinking coffee and contemplating your next move. These are all signs that you are not alone, even if it feels that way in the physical world.

Connecting with your angels and listening to your intuition requires a lot of trust - a trust in the unknown and the unseen. It requires discernment to distinguish between an intuitive hit and an ego-driven fear, both of which can have similar sensations in the body. Our body has an incredible in-built survival mechanism to keep us safe. Our nervous system alerts us to danger - as does our intuition. A gut feeling could be your nervous system responding to a genuine threat – or a perceived threat arising from thought – or intuition speaking to you.

Learning to trust your intuition is about learning to trust yourself, something that is conditioned out of you in childhood, typically through parenting and education as you learn to look to adults for answers. It's a process of remembrance as you re-connect with what is innate yet forgotten. It's distinguishing between the voice of your ego and the voice of your soul.

I do not doubt that intuition was guiding me through my difficult times. I didn't necessarily listen, and if I had, I can't say that I would have taken immediate action, but when I was ready, the angels were there.

Surrendering is a big part of learning to trust. Our fears drive the need to control, yet we can only control ourselves. When we let go of the need to control anything outside of us - people and circumstances - we surrender and in doing so drop out of our head and into our heart, creating a space for our intuition to speak. When we are in that space, we are more open to the messages from the angels. The fog clears, light shines through, and we experience clarity, peace of mind and stillness.

## How to Overcome Fear:

One of the greatest barriers to trust is fear. Fear speaks loudly and often leaves us doubting ourselves and our intuition, no matter how strong our intention to lean into trust. Fear can leave us paralysed and afraid to move forwards, however, freedom always awaits on the other side.

**When fear grips** you for no apparent reason take a few moments of quiet and ask yourself what has triggered the fear. Often, a past negative experience has left an imprint of unresolved emotion that is triggered by something as innocuous as a smell or familiar place. Other times, we're consumed by fearful thoughts or memories which elicit the fear response in our body. If you are able, identify the reason (without over-analysing), acknowledge and accept the feeling, and allow the fear to pass through you and subside. You may find a simple act of normality is all that is needed to shift your state. Maybe you just need to grab a healthy snack or a drink or go for a walk. Sharing your fears with people you trust is a perfect way to set the energy in motion so that it shifts and loses its hold on you, allowing you to come back home to yourself.

**In a flight response**, your body is protecting you by telling you to get away from a situation or a person that is causing you stress and anxiety. The best way is to safely extract yourself from the problem or person. I often hear people say, "Oh, I didn't want to upset them by being rude and leaving." My advice here is simple: turn the sentence around in your head and make the decision that you don't want to upset yourself by being in the company of the person. Honour your needs, particularly your own need for safety. Sometimes, we may overreact, and this is a time for self-reflection and discerning whether the fear is warranted. But, tune in and trust yourself. We have an in-built warning system for a reason! If you've experienced an abusive relationship, the lines between what is real and what isn't become blurred; sense of safety is distorted and heightened. It takes time to learn to trust yourself again and to tune into all the signals from your body, but it's essential that you learn to prioritise your own feelings of safety.

**Feel the fear** and do it anyway. Often, we really want to do something but are too scared of the outcome or the act of doing it. I would say to anyone who has ever felt like this that it's completely normal! No one got a medal by shying away from fear; life will always throw us curveballs and we either catch them or dodge them. Of course, there is a lot of unconscious thought and memory that we have little awareness of, but much of our fear comes our conscious thought in the moment. So, what if we could have those thoughts and do the thing regardless? Sometimes we just need to get out of our own way.

## LET'S REFLECT:

- Intuition never lies.
- Learning to trust your intuition is about learning to trust yourself.
- When you let go of the need to control anything outside of you, you surrender.
- Freedom is waiting on the other side of your fear.

"What's wrong with me?" cried the woman in pain,
Life had knocked her again and again.

"I can't sleep, yet I'm exhausted" said the man to his
wife,
Not recognising what had become of his high-flying
life.

"Please try and eat," pleaded the mother to her child.
Where had she gone, my daughter so wild?

Chronic Fatigue looked down on them all,
Knowing without doubt they would crumble and
fall.

"Sticks and commodes are a part of our life,"
Sobbed the man as he lay in the arms of his wife.

Feeling defined by the dreaded M.E.
All of them broken for the world to see.

"No," she screamed back, "I won't lose myself."
She wasn't ready to put her life on the shelf.

"I will survive, I will redefine.
I will not be yours; my life will be mine."

So pacing and meds and learning to walk,
Making herself eat and learning to talk.

Using the props the sticks and a chair,

Listening to others was so good to share.

"You're doing so well, you seem really fit."
She replied with a smile, "it's *my* M.E and I define
*it.*"

**– I Won't Be Defined**

4.

# COMING HOME

*"Happiness cannot be travelled to, owned, earned, worn or consumed. Happiness is the spiritual experience of living every minute with love, grace and gratitude."* ~ Denis Waitley

**W**hen you've experienced challenging or traumatic times, it can be hard to believe that you'll find happiness again. The truth is, the happiness that you seek is already within you, waiting to be found; sometimes you just need a little help to find it. When we look inside ourselves, we find love. We find our true self. And we come home.

2010 was a year of healing and re-building my life. I rented a house with the children and our relationship with their father slowly started to heal. My dad did his best to be involved in my children's lives in any way he could, assuming a 'fatherly' role and devoting his time and attention so that they felt loved and appreciated. However, I still felt that I lived too close to my ex. There was always a chance that I could bump into him. I didn't feel safe. I decided to move away from the area and rented a beautiful, quaint cottage. For the first time in years, I felt peaceful and at home.

Once the deeper wounds had started to heal, I felt ready to step into the dating world again. I wanted a companion, someone to share my life with; I didn't want to be alone. I joined the online dating site *Plenty of Fish* without much luck. Several months passed and I hadn't been on any dates so concluded that maybe it wasn't for me after all. One weekend in May 2011, I decided to cancel my membership.

As I was logging on, I saw a profile of a man I had been looking at for a couple of months, and I could see he was online. By this point, the angels were getting louder, and I'd been talking to them for some time, especially through my period of healing. Instead of closing my account, I was guided to click "hello", and moments later received a "hello" back. It turns out that he too had been about to log off at the precise moment that I contacted him, and later I was to find out that he had been looking at my profile picture as well.

We started chatting online, and I suggested that we meet for a coffee. "I'd love to," he said, "but I'm a bit bashed up at the moment." *Was this another fob-off?* I thought. I wasn't sure if I could handle any more rejection. As it happens, he was telling the truth, and it was a truth much closer to home than I realised!

Apparently he was covered in cuts and bruises after falling off his mountain bike into the bushes. "I was on my bike the other day down Sharlston Lane, and some lady with blonde hair in a green car on her phone whizzed past, and I fell off my bike!" he said.

*Oh, no!* I thought as the realisation dawned on me. Surely not? How was I going to break that to him? We were getting on so well …

"Erm…" I said, sheepishly, "What time was this?"

It turned out that that woman with the blonde hair in her green car was me! Yes, you heard that right – I'd nearly killed this man before we even met! Luckily, he saw the funny side and was very forgiving.

When we met up we clicked straight away. I felt very comfortable in his company. There were no awkward silences or pretence; I could be myself without any fear of judgment. We walked around a local beauty spot called New Millerdam. Before long we were holding hands; it felt the most natural thing in the world. I felt instantly safe with him. When he leaned in for a kiss and I reciprocated, it felt like home. After our walk we went for a brew in a café. Neither of us wanted to finish the date but I had shopping to do and hungry teenagers to feed. He came with me, and then I took him to my home and introduced him to Daisy and Edward. After the previous relationship, this was a massive step for me (and them), but it felt right.

We talked all night. It felt so good to have someone to listen and hold space for me. He was such a kind, gentle and sensitive man who happily drank tea with me all night. I opened up about my relationship history and my fears around dating again. He was profoundly spiritual, so I felt seen and understood. *Finally*, someone who got me, and this someone was my Rob, a kind gentle man with a loving soul who had been hurt countless times in the past. Together we went on a journey of healing. From then on, our relationship bloomed. I introduced him to my parents, but naturally, they were reluctant to welcome him with open arms. They took a long time to warm to him, fearing he would turn out like the others and hurt me, but warm to him they did.

Of course, in the nature of being human and none of us being infallible, it wasn't all a bed of roses. Rob was bi-polar, and loving a man with extreme mood swings has its challenges! It was a real test of unconditional love on my part, learning to deeply and truly love someone for who they are beneath their behaviour, while also ensuring that I wasn't trying to fix or save him in any way, instead accepting who he is, warts and all.

Six-weeks into our relationship I was given some devastating news: I had M.E. (Myalgic Encephalomyelitis).

I'd woken up one day with a terrible pain in my leg. It felt like walking through treacle. The pain spread to my back and wouldn't go away. After a while, I couldn't bear it any longer. I visited my GP for blood tests, yet all the results were in the normal range. Eventually, I was referred to the ME clinic who made the diagnosis. I couldn't understand it. "Why have I got this? I'm happy!" I said. My life was back on track, I was happier than I'd ever been and now … it felt as though the Universe was playing some sick joke! The physician turned to look at me. "It's because of emotional trauma," she said.

I thought 2010 was my year of healing, but in hindsight I realised that I was in fight-or-flight. The stress and trauma stagnated deep in my body and when I met Rob, he was the trigger for it all to come out. Feeling happier and more relaxed, my nervous system calmed, and the unresolved emotions found their way back up to the surface, much like a geyser before it erupts.

I ended up in a wheelchair. I was too fatigued to clean my teeth and couldn't even touch my toes! Everything required too much effort and was too painful. I needed round-the-clock care and support, and Rob did just that! He took me to the hospital and accompanied me to all of my appointments; he was so good to me. Having someone that you're in a new relationship with cleaning your commode is both humbling and humiliating in equal measure, but he did. At any point, he could have left me, but he chose to stay. This was the moment that I knew it was true love.

When we disconnect from our soul, we disconnect from love, the source of who we all are. We are all love – it is our true nature. Yet many of us spend our lives on a quest to find what is already within us. We seek connection and safety externally to fill what we perceive to be a deep void, yet the more we seek love and the more heartache we experience, the more the hole widens and deepens, further separating us from who we really are.

It is human nature to want to love and to be loved. Connection is one of the most basic and fundamental of human needs. We are sociable by nature, no matter how introverted we may be; we want to belong. We look for commonality and familiarity. We don't want to be outcast or ostracised from our families and communities. The threat alone is enough to keep us playing small or masking many aspects of our self; rejection only exacerbates deeply ingrained beliefs of not being good enough. It's one of the reasons we can become attached to abusive relationships – better to be with someone and belong somewhere than risk being alone.

When our sense of safety is threatened in our relationships we build armour around our hearts to protect us. This can either stop us from allowing love and avoiding intimacy, or we react to the pain by projecting our hurts in our relationship, even unconsciously entering relationships that align with our beliefs that we are not worthy of love.

The more we connect with our soul, the more we connect to the love that resides there. We realise our worth and recognise that nothing outside of us can give us the feeling that we seek. Of course, sometimes it takes the love, patience and belief of someone outside of us to help us find it within ourselves (and that's ok). While I do believe that we need to love ourselves first to realise that we are worthy and deserving of love, I do not advocate that we have to love ourselves in order to be loved. We are all lovable as we are. *You* are lovable as you are. You've simply forgotten and have to go through a process of relearning and remembering. And if it means allowing the love of a good partner or friend (or even the kindness of a stranger) to remind you, then so be it!

After the end of my first marriage and the trauma of my second, I didn't believe I was worthy of love. I couldn't help but internalise the shame and failure of both relationships. By the time I signed up for online dating, I'd been through a process of healing. I'd slowly started to rebuild all of the broken pieces of myself and, while there was still a long way to go, I felt much better about myself. I hadn't planned to meet anyone new; it was more for fun. Yet when Rob came along, it was as though he came at a time that was meant to be. I believe that, for all those times that our paths crossed in the past but we didn't meet, it was for a reason. Had I met Rob during my darkest years, I daresay I would have been too caught up in my inner chaos and circumstances to have noticed him. The angels gifted us to each other at a time that we were both ready; we both had to travel our own paths and walk our own stories – no matter how tumultuous – to get to the point that we could finally meet. We both had to come home to ourselves to come home to each other.

## How to learn to love yourself

We're all programmed for self-loathing, our inner critic driving a lot of our thought processes (and much of it unconsciously), which shapes how we interact with the world around us. Our relationship with self impacts our behaviours, how we show up in the world, and how we treat ourselves and others (and also what we tolerate from others). When we form a deeper connection with self, we have a deeper understanding, learn to trust ourselves and listen to our intuition. We have stronger personal boundaries, become better at communicating our wants and needs, and our relationships are improved. We also stop esteeming ourselves through our relationships, knowing that we are worthy at the core of our being. Of course, many of us have years of conditioning to reverse and reprogramme, so this isn't something that can be achieved overnight. But by taking baby steps, notice how much better you start to feel about yourself and how the quality of your life improves (even if your circumstances don't).

**Nobody is responsible for your happiness** – you are. Likewise, you're not responsible for anyone else's (or their anger and frustrations). Equally, be aware of how your actions *do* have an impact. You're not responsible for how others perceive or react to you, but actions and words *do* hurt, and it's okay to acknowledge when you've felt hurt too. Use your voice, have boundaries, but don't give your power away by making others responsible for your feelings: own them. We cannot control what happens outside of us, but we do have the power to choose how we respond.

**Show yourself kindness and compassion.** Allow yourself to make mistakes, knowing that every mistake is an opportunity to learn. Give yourself time and space to grow – life isn't a race to the finish line. Talk to yourself – and treat yourself – how you would your best friend. Befriend yourself. Every time you look in the mirror or glimpse your reflection, acknowledge that you're your best, most loyal companion who is always with you wherever you go. Take care of your body, mind and spirit. Meet all of your needs – eat healthily, move more, drink more water, do all the small things to show care for yourself.

**Own your past and your pain.** You don't have to be happy all the time. Honour each and every emotion as it arises and don't beat yourself up for not being happy, or justifying why you "should" be happy. You're human, you feel emotions. It's part of the human experience to have moods and emotions that ebb and flow. Be honest about your dark and messy parts, those you try to hide – your flaws are part of what makes you *you* so accept and own them. Own your regrets and mistakes. No human is perfect, everyone makes mistakes and has skeletons in their closet. Bring those skeletons out of the closet and release all shame attached to them. Trace your life all the way back from childhood so that you can understand every action, thought and behaviour you've ever had and show compassion to your younger self for not knowing any better, and doing her best with the limited knowledge and resources she had at the time.

---

## LET'S REFLECT:

1.  Happiness is an inside job – sometimes you need a little help to find it.
2.  The feeling of 'home' is your connection to your true essence – to soul, to spirit, to the divine. Surround yourself with the people and places that evoke this feeling within you.
3.  No matter how many times you've been hurt, love is available to you.
4.  You are deserving of love – allow yourself to receive it.

5. You do not need to love yourself to be loved – a loving soul will love you regardless and will help you find the love within yourself.

You are beautiful
You are bold
You bring forth the sunshine
Shining bright for me to hold

Your strength is infectious
Your strength is stealth
Your strength gives me reason
To believe in myself

We work together finding my truth
We work together on spiritual growth
We work together finding my path
Making me whole living my oath

You in my life like bees and nectar
You in my life like flowers in spring
You in my life always my ear
You in my life finding my voice to sing

*– You In My Life*

5.

# FOLLOWING THE BREADCRUMBS

*"You have to grow from the inside out. None can teach you, none can make you spiritual. There is no other teacher but your own soul." ~ Swami Vivekananda*

**L**ife is not linear, but culturally we are given the message that it is: you go to school, get a job, get married, buy a house and have children, in that order a bunch of very clear milestones and expectations. We often esteem ourselves through the boxes that we manage to tick, then berate ourselves or feel shame for those we don't. But what if life isn't linear? What if life is one great scribbly mess of twists and turns, ups and downs, calm and chaos? What if everything we experience, in whatever order, still leads us to where we are meant to be?

After shutting down my spirituality as a child, it slowly began to open up again when I had my son, Edward. Children are incredible for waking us up and cracking us open in many ways, whether it be forcing us to face our hidden wounds, or helping us to reconnect with and express our true nature.

Edward was born by c-section, so I spent the first three weeks simply holding him and connecting with him. Once walking became comfortable, I started meeting other mums for coffee. "Your baby's a little healer," I recall one of the mums saying.

By this point, my mum had started doing aromatherapy and reiki, and I was becoming more and more interested. My spirituality, having shut it down since my teens, was being re-ignited. When Edward was three, my friend Alex sent me a pack of Angel oracle cards from Australia. It's like she saw something in me that I couldn't see (or didn't want to see). Although a little part of me wanted to remain cynical, I loved them! I would ask questions to the cards to see what came through. Eventually, I was hooked. I'd take them everywhere with me, pulling cards for the children and my mum. I felt deeply connected to the angels; if I was the CEO, they were my team of advisors! During my darkest time I thought the angels had turned their back on me. The truth is, a part of me lost faith, and it was I who turned my back on them. The cards were soon forgotten and collected dust while I resumed 'normal' life.

Once I met Rob, I started to think about them again.

Rob being very spiritually open, we'd spend hours in deep conversation. The old, familiar knowing deep in my soul stirred again.

After I was diagnosed with M.E., life became more challenging. I couldn't just bounce out of bed to go to work anymore. Everything - every movement, every breath - became an effort. "Jane, you can't work with this condition. Why don't you start making jewellery?" my dad suggested one day.

It seemed the perfect solution. I wouldn't have to go anywhere; my hands were nimble (for now). The message I heard was use it or lose it. Indulging in something creative sounded like it could be therapeutic, so good for my overall wellbeing. Only, there was one problem.

"I don't know how to make jewellery," I said.

"We'll give you £200. Buy what you need and learn," Dad said.

I started making earrings and bracelets. Before long word got around and people started asking for custom-made items. I was enjoying this new-found creativity. I'd found something that not only brought me so much joy, but it also gave me a sense of purpose, especially on the difficult days.

By now, Daisy was at university while Edward was about to move to Brighton. My days were spent making jewellery, and I was starting to embrace a more spiritual life, but I was missing my children. The house felt quiet and empty without them. I needed something more. I had an angel alter and one day, holding my oracle cards, I sent a prayer up to heaven.

"Show me what to do. I'm open. Show me."

I lit a candle. Almost immediately after, a friend messaged another friend who lived in America on Facebook: "Can you get me one of these cheaper than 40 dollars?" It was an Archangel Raphael bracelet made of clear Quartz, moss agate and Tibetan silver.

"Can't Jane Dunning make it?" my friend replied.

"No, she doesn't make that sort of thing."

I took this as a sign. I made the bracelet, sold it to my friend, then got to work making more archangel bracelets using crystals and gemstones. I set up a stall in my local indoor market and soon expanded to make holistic jewellery and sourced fair-trade spiritual gifts and silver jewellery. They sold like hotcakes! Before long, I branched out and created different bracelets for different archangels – I was even featured in Spirit and Destiny magazine.

In 2016 I met a very spiritual lady through my stall. She invited me to her house and asked me to bring my cards and to give her a reading. Well, I wasn't expecting the reading to be so accurate! It's as though the message came through me from somewhere higher. I felt so at home and at peace giving her the reading, as though I'd been doing it all my life. She told me that I could do it for a living. Something cracked open inside me, like a massive beacon of light had illuminated me from the inside.

I went for a reading at a local Mind Body Spirit event. The medium looked at me as though someone had kicked him from behind.

"Why have I got Archangel Metatron kicking me in the back?" he asked. I smiled. I'd been looking at Archangel Metatron only that morning. This was another sign. I wanted to become an angelic reiki healer but lacked confidence in my abilities. "You've got all the tools now, get on and do it!" the medium said. He was right. These gifts weren't new to me; I'd been practising them for much of my life without even realising. And even when I closed myself off to spirituality, they never left me. They were simply waiting to be reawakened.

10-minutes after the reading, the phone rang. It was my friend Todd in America, who very rarely called. I told him about the reading, and he gave me the extra little push and encouragement I needed to take action. So, I headed home, jumped onto the internet, and found an angelic reiki master. I booked an appointment to become attuned to angelic reiki. Again, money was a barrier. My dad loaned me the money for the attunement. "We want you to be happy and make a success of your life," he said. I will be eternally grateful to my parents for the love and support that they've always shown.

By the end of the year, I was a qualified angelic reiki healer and am now a reiki master. The peace, joy and beauty of reiki is breathtaking. Never in my life have I felt so complete; I know this is what I was born to do. I still create jewellery, only now I can attune them with reiki healing energy so that they're extra potent and special. I've received incredible feedback from customers in the UK and America, praising the quality of the jewellery and the inert angelic energy they feel as they open the package. Many have mentioned that they feel a deep, authentic connection to their angel when wearing the bracelet. Rob turned our spare room into a healing room. It is a beautiful sanctuary of peace and serenity. My dreams have come true all because I tuned into the signs and the guidance that the angels were giving me.

When I look back at my life, I can see the breadcrumbs that lead me to exactly where I was meant to be. Even the difficult times brought me here; they were part of the plan. Without my darkest moments, I may never have re-connected with the angels. Without the abuse in my relationship, I may never have developed the courage to leave. If I'd never left, I might never have met Rob and learnt the true meaning of love. When I connect the dots, it's as though nothing happened by accident; the Universe, God, the angels - whatever the semantics - were paving the way so that I would get to where I am today, like a perfectly orchestrated series of events to jolt me from my slumber. In fact, Rob and I have traced back to when we were 13 years old when our paths crossed for the first time. It would be many more times of near-misses before we finally met.

I'm not saying I deserved any of my experiences – I certainly don't subscribe to the idea that 'there are no victims', a widespread belief in many spiritual circles. There are many situations and circumstances that we as humans are a victim to, and we need to acknowledge that. We cannot control others or their actions towards us, or indeed know the path that they are on or the lessons they are here to learn. But I do believe that every experience brought with it a profound lesson for my soul's evolution and - more importantly - brought me closer to my gifts and authentic self-expression. Would I be doing what I am now, living the dream and feeling so at home and at peace with myself had I not experienced pain? It's not possible to say. But I do know this: my experiences shaped me; they allowed me to find my inner strength and resilience and remember who I am.

It's easy to get frustrated or discouraged when we feel we're not at the place we want to be in our lives. Perhaps we haven't got the relationship, the career or the money that we expected to have by now, what with our mental checklists and egoically-defined path. However, when we look back at our lives, we are reminded of how far we've come. If we hold on to any anger, bitterness or resentment towards our lived experiences, we stay stuck in the past. When we're not where we desire to be, we're thrust into a non-existent future, developing anxiety and overwhelm as we push ourselves onto a path that was perhaps never intended for us. When we can see the ways that we grew from our past experiences and the lessons we learned, then we can start to believe that perhaps they were for our highest good (even though they certainly wouldn't have felt that way at the time). We can see that we are on the right path, and always were; we start to trust that things will happen when they need to.

By connecting with our angels - whether by using oracle cards or praying, for example - we can get clear guidance on the steps we need to take. The more we listen, the more the path will naturally unfold. The stars will align, more coincidences will seemingly happen, and more of what your soul desires will come into your awareness. Opportunities will present themselves, the right people will come into your life at the right time, and a lot of the heaviness and exhaustion (that we typically experience when our soul is unexpressed) begins to shift. We feel lighter. We feel more at peace. And any challenges become much easier to navigate.

## How to Connect with the Angels

Even if you cannot see angels physically, they are there, leaving signs to communicate with you. Even if you don't consider yourself particularly spiritual or, up until now, haven't given angels much thought, they are here to help you so long as you do your part to connect with them. The angels are available to you to guide you through any adversity or challenges you face in your life.

**Pay attention** to any physical sensations you feel and take note of changes in your surroundings. Perhaps the air temperature around you suddenly drops, or you notice goosebumps on your skin. Maybe you can feel an unexplained presence nearby. You may even feel something lightly brush your skin.

**Observe repeating numbers**. Seeing 11:11 is an especially angelic number and means that your angels are trying to send you a divine message. The more you see repeating numbers, the stronger the connection between you and your angels. When you see these numbers, particularly 1s, know that the angels are nearby. Observe your thought process in that moment – perhaps these numbers are giving you the answer.

**Before you go to bed**, ask the angels to appear in your dreams. Send out a loving message, asking that you wish to meet them in your dreams, or ask a specific question that you'd like them to answer. They may not appear that night, but they will make their presence known to you over the coming days.

## LET'S REFLECT:

- Your life is a trail of breadcrumbs that has led you to exactly where you're meant to be right now.

- Your experiences don't define you, but they have shaped who you are.
- By connecting with your angels, you can get clear guidance on how to move forward.
- Your angels are available to you so long as you are open and willing to connect with them.
- When you look back at your life, you are reminded of how far you've come.

The smell of the sports hall, the quiet of the gym
My favourite moment before the dancers come in

Point your toes and stretch up high
Jump as if you want to fly

The competition's drawing near
The show is nearly done
It's been hard to teach and lots of tears
But mostly it's been fun

The moment that you see the dance play out
You cheer, you cry, you clap and shout

The dancers are so perfect
They are loving what they do
They know it's because you cherished them
They know it's down to you

*– Dancing*

# 6.

# ESCAPING REALITY

*"Dance is the hidden language of the soul." ~ Martha Graham*

Our soul speaks to us in many ways, yet we are so consumed by our thinking that we barely notice. Having a creative outlet helps to drop out of our head and into our body and heart space, connecting to our inner being and giving respite from the stresses that preoccupy us. For me, that outlet was dance.

In 1980 I danced in a contemporary dance group ran by a local mum. I absolutely adored it! I loved all the costumes, the way I could move my body with wild abandon, the way all worries and thoughts melted away as soon as I was on that floor. In short: I felt alive.

When I danced, I felt like a ballerina, yet soon learnt that any notion of me actually becoming one were far beyond my capabilities. I was too big and fat, or at least that's what I was told by the man who ran the group. Up until that point, I had no real awareness of self-image. I knew I loved to move, I loved to dance … and that was it! I never once felt that I couldn't do it, that I shouldn't. Until that scathing remark, that is.

I watched the other competitors from the sideline and cried my eyes out. I desperately wanted to be on the dance floor. So, I moved to another group who were more accepting (and who wanted me to dance) and stayed there happily for a few years. Before long I was 'too old' and had to retire from competing. My dad suggested I set up my own group so that I could teach.

I was determined to teach, so I did. I wanted to show other girls that their weight or body-shape need not be a barrier to them wanting to express themselves through dance. I wanted to show them that they didn't have to conform to societal standards of beauty. I've had an on-off relationship with food my entire life and even had a gastric band fitted in my 30s (subsequently removed when I started throwing up blood due to eating through it). So teaching became the natural next step.

With Dad's support and encouragement, I set up my own contemporary dance group. We taught together; it was so much fun. Teaching children to dance filled me with the same level of aliveness as when I myself was dancing. And for the girls and boys, it gave them a sanctuary.

Every child who walked through my door and onto the dance floor could be themselves entirely. They could lose themselves in the music and the moves, freeing themselves and their minds from any worries and troubles. No matter what shit they were going through, this was their safe place. They got to experience that feeling of joy, and for those 4-minutes during a performance, they were seen, really seen, and acknowledged and appreciated for who they are.

The group ran incredibly successfully until 2004 when I moved to Yorkshire and had to shut it down. I was heartbroken, not just for myself but also for the members who attended. But it's what I had to do. Once we moved, I found another group in Sheffield and Daisy joined me, having been dancing herself since she was five-years-old.

When my first husband came out as gay, I sought solace in the group. There were some male teachers who were gay who helped me to come to terms with his sexuality. I felt able to talk to the children more openly about gay men as they had other points of reference. For so long I'd beaten myself up about the fact I hadn't seen any signs, more so that he'd been suffering in silence. What kind of wife was I not to notice? But I came to realise that, while some men wear their sexuality on their sleeves, others don't, and you simply cannot tell. This really helped the children and me.

In 2007, my second husband (of all people) approached my dad. "Why don't you set up a dance troop for Jane to teach?" So, he did. Together they found a hall and got all of the props needed to begin the group then let me in on their little secret, telling me to think of a name. Whether it was just another way for my second husband to have control over and play the 'perfect husband' role me I don't know, but whatever his intentions, I'm glad he suggested it! Daisy was still dancing at the Sheffield group but from time-to-time she helped me out. Before long it became a real family business. Even Edward was a part of it, as he'd been dancing himself since 8-years-old (and subsequently, now as an adult, has started a new life in Brighton with a girl who he met from his dancing days).

When I was diagnosed with M.E., I had to step back a little. I was less mobile and couldn't always think clearly: I had intense brain fog and struggled to find the words at times. Daisy stepped up and took the reins, assuming the role as the main director of the group. She was brilliant! Meanwhile, I could attend the competitions in my wheelchair, clapping my hands and cheering the dancers on. I could still give instruction to the members – the beauty of it being a family business! It really was a dream come true. It kept my mind (and soul) alive! From those earlier days of not being able to compete because I was 'too fat' to now still joining in while in a wheelchair – I was having the last laugh! The best bit? We'd created such a welcoming, inclusive and nurturing environment, exactly what motivated me to teach in the first place, and to this day (even though I'm no longer teaching), the group is still achieving so much success.

When teaching, the girls and boys would call me Jane. I wasn't accustomed to hearing 'Mum' in that environment. My daughter would get frustrated with this. "Mum," she'd say, trying to get my attention. "Mum! Mum! Mum!" But I'd ignore her, completely oblivious. One day, she tried a different approach. "Jane," I heard in my right ear. It was Daisy. She'd figured out how to get my attention, at last! This became a bit of an in-joke for several years, Daisy regularly calling me Jane because it became natural in that environment while at home I was 'Mum'. Eventually, after ignoring her at home one day and Daisy addressing me as 'Jane' to get my attention. That was a big no, no! Our mother/daughter relationship was as treasured as our Jane/Daisy relationship at dance. I've cherished every moment in the group with Daisy, Edward and my dad – and all of the gorgeous, creative (and sometimes lost) souls that have embraced the dance floor – the best years of my life! Being there for them, dancing them, leading them – they don't know how much they saved me.

My family has slowly stepped away from the group, my daughter now working in her dream job and prioritising her career, and my son relocating to the South coast, but our legacy lives on. I still act as chair – a way for me to dip my toes in and still experience the joy of being involved in such an incredible group – but other people have picked up the reins. Stepping away has come at the perfect time. By leaving the group, I've freed up space which has allowed my spirituality to flourish and grow. The angels have more room to communicate as my mind isn't as busy, the messages are clear, I have much clearer direction in my life and business, feel more connected to my purpose and … this book has been born. Everything has lined up perfectly since I paid attention, listened, and took aligned action.

## How to connect with your creativity

Despite what messages you may have received throughout your life, you are creative. You are a creative being born from creation itself with an infinite capacity to create something from nothing. The energy of your soul that makes you feel alive is the same creative energy that can help you make decisions and consciously create your life. Every time you've solved a problem, cooked something from scratch or put pen to paper, you've demonstrated creativity. Not being artistically talented does not mean you're not creative – too many people have blocked their creative flow by thinking this.

**Indulge in a creative hobby.** Whether you take a painting class, join a dance or knitting group or start cookery lessons, the more you tap into your creativity, the more your creativity will open up. The more it opens up, the more you'll start to see new opportunities and possibilities present themselves. Hobbies can get you into a meditative state, so your angels and intuition have more space to come through – and are also a great way to meet new people and have fun!

**Having a creative outlet** is a powerful tool for mental wellbeing. Through creativity we can express our inner world, connect with our inner being, and process and heal some of our negative experiences. If you don't yet have a self-care ritual, consider incorporating something creative as part of your routine.

**Dance** is a fantastic way to shift your state and increase your vibration, particularly when you're feeling blue. You don't have to join a dance class to dance – why not invest in a disco light and have a kitchen disco? Put your favourite tune on full blast, sing at the top of your lungs, move your body, and notice your energy lift. This is a great thing to do with children too to shift their energy. Dance with your partner, feeling the movement together. This can be incredibly healing as you connect at soul level with the ones you love.

## LET'S REFLECT:

- You are a creative being with an infinite potential to create.
- Having a creative outlet helps you to connect to your inner being and escape the stresses of life.
- Consider creativity as a tool for self-care and mental wellbeing.
- Creativity can create space to allow your angels and intuition to come through.

It's okay to grieve, it's okay to cry.
There is no right or wrong way to feel
When our loved ones die.

After the anger and tears and pains,
We slowly open our eyes to see and realise that all
the love remains.

We feel them in our souls in everything we knew.
We know they're only a breath away and watching
what we do.

So cry today but celebrate your loved ones very dear.
But know tomorrow and all your days they are
watching you, always near.

*– Grief*

7.

# CUPCAKES ARE SLIMMING

*"What children need most are the essentials that grandparents provide in abundance. They give unconditional love, kindness, patience, humour, comfort, lessons in life. And, most importantly, cookies." ~ Rudy Giuliani*

**G**rief is a process and part of the human experience, yet many of us avoid it because it feels too painful. Whether a pet or a loved one dies, or you're letting go a part of your life that has shaped your entire identity, grief is inevitable and can help us grow in many ways.

"What do you mean, Nan? Cupcakes aren't slimming!" It was the early 80's and Nanny Pat had joined a slimming club. "They are if I count the points," she said. My nan had always had a sweet tooth and I am sure it's where I got mine from. There was always pudding after dinner, biscuits in the biscuit tin, and whenever we went out shopping we would have to go to a café for a nice cup of tea and a slice of cake. It was the unwritten rule! Even now, whenever I choose a treat or find myself in a cake shop, I gravitate towards one of my nan's favourites – usually a vanilla slice or lemon meringue pie! And of course, Christmas wouldn't be Christmas without jelly sweets!

Life as a granddaughter was good. I was the only one for seven years until cousins started to be born. Nan adored my boy cousins, but I wanted to believe that I was the most special, what with being the eldest. On my father's side I had to learn to share my grandparents with other girls, which at first wasn't easy. To say I wasn't used to sharing the attention is an understatement! However, I adored the babies and, being seven years older, I was in charge and was always made to feel important. My relationship with Nanny Pat on my mother's side was always going to remain. The bond we shared was instant. With my parents being so young when I was born, Nanny Pat was always on hand to give advice and support, right up to the day she passed. She was an authority on life, babies, children and teenagers. Whenever life threw me a curveball, I would turn immediately to my Nan; her words of wisdom still echo in my soul. We were close friends and I can recall some wonderful memories and stories spanning over 50 years.

One time, Nan wanted to go shopping but had

recently undergone a knee replacement so couldn't walk. I suggested a mobility scooter which seemed the perfect solution – Nan was far too proud to be pushed in a wheelchair and I figured she'd prefer to travel around in style! Only, there was a flaw to my plan: Nan wasn't a driver in any shape or form. We'd been around all of the shops and to the café for cake without any trouble when Nan decided she wanted to buy Easter eggs for the children. "Let's go to Woolworths," I suggested. It was only outside, and as Nan's first venture on her scooter had been without issue thus far, I reasoned one more shop wouldn't do any harm. Nan too was feeling confident. "I'm just going to go over here ," I said as we entered the shop, "back in a minute." Well, no sooner was my back turned than I heard an almighty crash followed by commotion behind me. I turned around and there was Nan, suppressing a laugh, her scooter planted into what had been a huge display of stacked up Easter eggs, albeit they were now scattered all over the floor (and her!). "Just drive forward," I said, tears of laughter running down my face. So she did … straight back into the eggs! We couldn't contain ourselves, laughing hysterically as we left the shop, a trail of chocolate eggs behind us. We laughed about this for many years, and it was many more years before she would use another mobility scooter. Needless to say, her reversing skills never improved!

I loved our shopping trips. Nan enjoyed me helping her buy clothes, telling me I had an eye for what looked good. One of Nan's favourite things was to buy clothes for the children. "I can't take my money with me," she'd always say. She wanted to spoil us all while she was still alive. The last birthday present my nan gave me before she passed was the Angelic Reiki treatment I had before my attuning – the best £30 she ever spent on me because it changed my life forever!

Nan loved babies and when I had my children, she spent many hours helping me. She only lived a mile down the road and was always on hand for advice and babysitting duties. But, of course, we can't have birth without death. Eventually the day came when I had to say a final goodbye to my beloved nan. She celebrated her 94th birthday and  two days later suffered a stroke. Six weeks later, on Mother's Day, my parents called me to tell me to come to the hospital as soon as I could. I already knew Nan was ready to pass. Walking into the room I could feel the Angels around Nan's bed. She looked very peaceful. Holding her hand, I spoke to her higher self ."It's time to go home," I said. "Your Angels are waiting for you, Nan." At 5.25 pm, as the sun shone and I held her hand, my nan went home. I felt her spirit flood me with unconditional love, unlike anything I had ever felt before. It was a beautiful death.

As I lay in bed that night, grief hit me, and it hit me hard. The most horrendous pain gripped me, like a huge blow in the centre of my chest. My nan. My beautiful nan, my rock, my best friend who had been such a monumental part of my life was gone. The emptiness was unlike anything I'd felt before. No words can do justice to how much I missed her (and still do). The following month I was a wreck. I couldn't work properly, healing was out of the question, and selling on my stall and dealing with customers was hard. So, to honour the pain, I allowed myself time to remember and reflect. Do we truly heal from grief? I don't think so. But we can acknowledge and honour each stage and keep the memories of those we have lost alive.

Grief is different for everyone; there is no right or wrong way to grieve. Sometimes we don't know how we are going to grieve until we are placed in a position where we have to. Sometimes we can hold it together, going about our lives and functioning as any other person, while other times we fall apart, often over the smallest of things.

I went through a period of grieving when my first marriage broke down. No one had physically died but my marriage had. It felt like everything that I'd built around it – my life, my entire identity – had died with it. But losing my nan felt different. I felt like I'd lost a limb and had to learn how to function without it. For a year, I couldn't move past this feeling of loss. I don't know at what point it changed, but over time I became more accepting of the loss. I found that my wins were her wins because I knew she would have been so proud of me; the more I achieved the more I felt I was honouring her memory. I know she would be incredibly proud of me for writing this book (and especially for reliving Scootergate!).

Going through intense change and growth can also force you to grieve as you shed the identity that you have created. Changing jobs, leaving relationships and even moving home can invoke deep feelings of sadness as you let go of everything you knew and all that has been familiar. When you're on a spiritual journey and letting go of all aspects of who you are – or who you think you are - the masks drop, all that has felt safe and familiar shatters, and a process of grief begins as you step closer to your true essence. The ego doesn't like change; any kind of transformation is a death of the ego, of sorts.

Death is a profound time of reflection as we evaluate our own lives, yet any desire to change is often short-lived . How often have you been so touched and impacted by a global tragedy, yet have resumed normal life the following day? Death reminds us that our physical existence is temporary – what better reason to live a more fulfilled and soul-aligned life.

## How to overcome grief

Grief isn't linear and has many stages. It doesn't have a timeframe, or a final destination, merely a moment of acceptance (which in itself can ebb and flow). Much like how the weather changes, you can experience four seasons of grief in one day. As much as you may want to push those feelings away, as with all emotions, honour them. Grief comes in waves – ride them.

**Don't let anyone** tell you how long you "should" grieve. Your grief belongs to you; you know when you're ready to accept it, even if you cannot fully move on. Honour every emotion as it arrives, feel it, and let it pass, knowing that the cycle of grief comes in waves and you'll likely feel this way again. Everything that you're feeling is okay. If you need to talk to someone professionally, don't be afraid to reach out to a grief counsellor, or someone who will just hold space for you to talk while they listen.

**Many people** fear death, so they struggle to know what to say. Don't be afraid to express what you need, whether it be someone to listen or maybe someone to bring normality into your life. Maybe you want people to be able to talk without awkwardness – let them know! And equally, if you need time and space, don't be afraid to communicate that too.

**You may experience grief** even though someone hasn't died, particularly if you are on a spiritual journey. The ego dies many deaths when we peel back the layers of trauma and conditioning. No one said healing would be easy! Honour what you feel. Know that these feelings will pass and are a normal part of the healing process.

## LET'S REFLECT:

- Grief is a cycle. It comes in waves. Honour every step of the process (even when it comes full circle again).
- There is no time limit to grief.
- There is no 'one way' to grieve. Own and acknowledge your own grief, even if it looks very different to someone else's.
- Death reminds us that physical existence is temporary – live your life now!

Don't look at me and think that I'm fat
Don't look at me and think that I'm thin
See past the shell and look at me
See the person who resides within

Food makes me feel good, it gives me a high
Food often makes me want to lay down and cry
Using the food to feed my pain
Eating and eating again and again

Starving and lying to those that I love
Praying for help from Him up above
Why do I do it, keep eating this food?
Does it help me? Or improve my mood?

*No, I don't think so* says the voice in my head
*So have a bath and take a good book to bed*

So don't look at me or tell me I'm fat
Don't point you finger or tell me I'm thin
Help me get healthy get a grip on my food
Love me, applaud me, be part of my win

**– Feeding My Soul**

## 8.

# FOOD FOR THE SOUL

"Our bodily food is changed into us, but our
spiritual food changes us into it." ~ Meister Eckhart

**O**ur relationship with food has a deep
spiritual and emotional connection.
When our spiritual and emotional
needs are not met, food can become our
emotional crutch or the tool to disconnect us
further from ourselves. Food addiction is lack of
connection – both human and spiritual – so we
seek to fill the void through food (or many other
substances and behaviours). The more we
connect with our soul, the less enslaved we are
by our often-disempowering food relationship.

I've battled with eating disorders for most of my adult
life and have spent years in counselling for it. In all
honesty, only since I've really embraced and
connected with the angels have I got a handle on it.
For many years I fed – or starved – my soul,
depending on an unmet need that food (or lack
thereof) fulfilled.

As a child I loved sweet food. My parents worried about this, often putting a limit on my eating. As a teenager I became a secretive eater of sweets and chocolate - especially through my scared and angry years – buying confectionary and hiding it in my room.

After my first marriage ended, I became anorexic. I couldn't eat or even hold down any food. I was so devastated and heartbroken by the split that I lost my appetite entirely. In hindsight, I realise that I struggled with his sexuality. A big part of me still didn't want to believe it, couldn't believe that he was a gay man. Food became hard to swallow; it made me feel sick. The reality was, I struggled to swallow the truth of everything that had happened.

By the time husband number two came along my weight had yo-yoed as I bounced between bingeing and deprivation. Over time, my weight crept up; my body couldn't handle the constant weight changes and my hormones were all over the place. But my new husband didn't seem to mind. He loved me as I was, or so I thought, until our honeymoon revealed his true nature and apparent disgust of me and my body.

In my thirties after having my children, I had a gastric band fitted. By this point my eating was out of control and I simply couldn't bear being at such an uncomfortable weight. So a gastric band seemed the perfect solution. And, for a while, it was. I ate minimal food but soon started to feel deprived – the psychology behind my eating hadn't been addressed and I started using food again to meet my emotional needs . Soon I was eating far more than the band would allow. At first I would vomit, the typical response to overeating with a band, but soon my stomach became accustomed to my increasingly larger portions and I'd manage to hold the food down. By my mid-forties, I ate so much that I ate through the band. I started coughing up blood and was rushed to hospital to have the band removed.

*** 

Our relationship with food has a deep spiritual and emotional connection. When we are unable to be present to our emotions, we typically turn to food. For others, alcohol, gambling, sex or shopping may be the emotional crutch. Sometimes we use food to stuff down all that we don't want to feel, literally using the food to physically push down our emotions. Sometimes we use food as a distraction or to numb us, focusing on the food and the process of eating so that we don't have to think our thoughts or feel our feelings. Other times, when we feel disconnected or unsafe, we use food to fill the gaping hole inside, the food becoming the tool to feel safe and connected. If we lack pleasure in our lives, food can fill the void – the food providing a dopamine hit and instant gratification … until the next fix. Sometimes when we're hungry we're hungry for something other than food, such as connection or adventure.

As well as being unable to swallow life experiences, as already mentioned, anorexia can be away of denying pleasure and fulfillment. Anorexia is often rooted in a feeling of not being good enough or deserving enough, and a deep desire to control aspects of self when everything else feels out of control.

At a soul level, food often provides nourishment when fulfillment does not. When you disconnect from your soul, don't be surprised if food (or some other substance) takes its place. How often do you eat because you're bored, for example? Boredom is disconnection from the soul and if you're on a path that isn't aligned to your soul, you may find that you frequently boredom eat (or drink). Our cravings can indicate a nutritional need, and can also communicate to us a deeper, soul yearning. A craving for sugary foods, for example, can indicate a craving for more sweetness in your life. Any time that you're out of your soul's alignment, it will manifest typically as food or eating related issues, or may manifest directly in your body. IBS (Irritable Bowel Syndrome), for example, has a deep mind-body connection and a spiritual one too. Gut issues can indicate an inability to "stomach" negative life experiences (or even life itself) and be a symptom of stress. Gut issues can also symbolise living a life that is out of alignment to your soul and a deep soul desire to express your unique gift and soul's purpose.

A nourished soul requires little physical sustenance. You may find the thing that makes you feel the most alive is the thing that has you losing all sense of time and hunger. Ever spent a whole day focused on something that lights you up, only to realise that you've unknowingly skipped breakfast and lunch? Ever experienced hunger, and when you've fulfilled that hunger with the very thing your soul yearned for, your physical hunger fades away?

One of the greatest ways for a soul to feel nourished is through contribution and the act of giving back over and above yourself. This need to contribute typically comes later on in life through maturity and evolution, and a deep soul yearning, and becomes blatantly obvious at a soul level if the need isn't met. Fulfillment meets both a spiritual and human need – the point at which our soul and human fully integrates. When this need becomes so strong, yet we are not doing anything to fulfil it, we often lack meaning, purpose and experience depression – or even a midlife crisis.

Our soul desires so much more than we are giving it. Quite often we want out of life altogether and to 'go home' because we feel tired – specifically, our soul feels tired – and again, food and alcohol in particular begin to fill the void.

## How to Feed Your Soul

**Observe the patterns** of your behaviour and your habits around food. Without judgement, notice the times that you're using food as an emotional crutch or a tool to bypass the needs of your soul. What other ways can you meet your needs? What other ways can you say yes to pleasure or your soul desires?

**Honour your feelings** around your body and food. Acknowledge any shame that you carry and sit with it until the feeling passes, knowing that you are safe and lovable as you are. Accept the times that you (perceive yourself to) make a poor food choice, or the times that you recognise that food is meeting an unmet need. Be present to your eating, and notice how a little mindfulness can take the guilt and power away. Know that much of the shame you carry around your body doesn't belong to you. Own the feeling, but energetically hand the 'baggage' back to the person whose own wounds and insecurities were projected onto you.

**Love yourself** for who you are. Move your body more, spend more time doing the things you love that have you feeling alive. Bring more joy and pleasure into your life. Nourish your soul with the people, places and hobbies that light you up. Evaluate the areas of your life that leave you feeling most disconnected and, if it's within your means to do so, make changes.

**Eat with heartfelt purpose**. If that means having cake, then have cake. Eat it. Love it. Feel into the experience with all of your senses. Enjoy without the guilt.

## LET'S REFLECT:

- Your cravings often communicate a deeper soul yearning
- One of the greatest ways for a soul to feel nourished is through contribution
- Stress, an inability to digest negative life experiences, and living out of soul alignment can lead to digestive issues e.g. IBS.

- Disconnection from our soul can manifest as physical symptoms, poor eating habits and disease.

# EPILOGUE

My journey has taken many twists, turns and adversities yet each experience allowed me to find an inner strength and resilience that saw me through and come out a truer, stronger and more soulful version of Jane. Through every experience, I called upon the angels to ask for help, and they never abandoned me, even when I turned my back on them.

As I went through my Reiki attunement, a message came through loud and clear: I had to forgive. I had to forgive my first husband for the hurt he caused, I had to forgive my second for the abuse and suffering, and I had to forgive myself and stop blaming myself. I also needed to accept everything that happened, past and present. And so, I did. Bit by bit, I found a way to forgive.

The wounds of trauma and pain can leave you with lasting feelings of anger and bitterness, especially when hurt by someone you love and trust. When we forgive, we are releasing the feelings of resentment, bitterness or anger towards another. When we cling onto those feelings and a deep sense of injustice, they eat away at us on the inside and can manifest as disease in the body. Forgiveness frees you from the shackles of the past; it brings you closer to inner peace. Of course, forgiveness doesn't invalidate the pain others have caused you. It doesn't make what they did okay. You may feel that they are not deserving of forgiveness, and that is ok. But it does free you to move forward in your life.

Forgiveness is for your own growth and happiness. When you hold on to the past, it harms you far more than it harms the offender. When you forgive, it frees you to live in the present. It improves your physical and mental wellbeing; the nervous system responds to negative emotion in detrimental ways. Forgiveness eliminates the negativity that results from hurt by releasing the emotion around it. You do not need to forget or condone any wrongdoing. Neither do you need to make amends with the person who caused you harm. Through the act of forgiveness, you reclaim your personal power. The act that hurt you might always be with you, but forgiveness can lessen its grip on you and free you from the invisible hold the offender has on you. Forgiveness can aid your spiritual growth, leading to understanding, empathy and compassion for the one who hurt you.

The biggest shift for me was joining a heart circle where I learned to truly connect to and open my heart and release a lot of the pain that resided there. I learnt to be present to my pain and emotions and, subsequently, become more present in my life which has enriched it no end! I learnt to celebrate my sexuality, my body, and love the true me, warts and all! I can now look into the mirror at myself and say, "I love you, Jane," and mean it.

Rob and I went wild camping for 8-days in Glastonbury. I spent the time reading, writing and being at one with nature, being fully present to myself and everything around me as old wounds began to resurface and heal. Rob sat by in close acceptance as I slowly stepped out of my cocoon of self-hatred. If there's just one message I want you to take away it's this: losing self-hatred isn't easy, but it can be done!

My life feels magical. I feel blessed to wake up every day and excited about what the day will bring. And when I have a tough day, I have everything I need to help me navigate them: the angels, faith and self-belief. I bought a campervan when I was 54, and when I turned 55 I didn't get one but two tattoos (which was incredibly liberating … and painful)! I get to play dress up at Viking festivals and aged 55 bought myself a bicycle with a basket. I'd had a romantic fantasy of buying bread to put in the basket and imagined myself cycling along like someone out of an 80s Flake advert. Needless to say, the long flowing skirt wasn't very practical, and I was far too shaky not to wear a helmet! But, in that short moment, another dream (no matter how small) became reality.

Life is fun! I feel connected to myself; my creativity is alive and my inner child is happy. I feel like me, the me that I'd buried and hidden for so long believing that I was inherently flawed. Well, now I know different. I still have wobbly days – I'm human after all – but I now know at the core of my very being that I am loved, lovable, safe and enough. *More* than enough.

**And so are you.**

I've always been there watching you
Cheering you on and holding you high
I've always been there loving you
Sending you joy and watching you fly

I've always been there comforting you
Your sadness mine when you fell by the way
I've always been there loving you
Sending you strength to get through the day

I've always been there teaching you
Sending the clues for you to find
I've always been there pushing you
Knowing the more I gave you would open up your mind

I've always been there healing you
Ensuring you never carried more than you could bear
I've always been there speaking quietly in your ear
Look towards the heavens, come and find me there

I will always be with you forever more
By your side I will stay
I will always be with you through all your journeys
Shining you bright in every way

*– My Angel on my Shoulder*

# ABOUT THE AUTHOR

Jane Dunning is an Author, Speaker, Angelic Reiki Master and creator of Archangel Jewellery who has gone from heartache, domestic abuse and an M.E. diagnosis to living a happy, healthy and blissful life.

Standing in front of her Angel alter one day, holding her beloved angel cards and asking for guidance, Jane had no idea what that moment would open up for her.

Since that day she has been on a journey of self-discovery, hope and blessings as the angels have guided her towards angelic enlightenment (and the man of her dreams!) to live a life filled with love, happiness and joy.

Jane now helps others connect with their angels while helping them find strength and inner peace through their challenges.

## CONNECT WITH JANE:

**Website:** www.jandre.co.uk

Jandre products enhance your life by bringing spiritual enrichment, love, happiness and blessings in a box – a little bit of me for you to keep.

**Email:** jane@jandre.co.uk

**Facebook:** @jandre

**Instagram:** jandre_uk

Connect with me on LinkedIn

Printed in Poland
by Amazon Fulfillment
Poland Sp. z o.o., Wrocław

64685806R00067